everyday Writing
Intervention Activities

MW00342666

Table of Contents

Using Everyday Writing Intervention Activities

Research shows that reading and writing are reciprocal processes, and often the same students who struggle as readers need support to develop their writing skills.

The Everyday Writing Intervention Activities provide developmentally appropriate, easy-to-use, five-day writing units for Grades K–5. Each unit focuses on a particular writing process or writer's craft skill and provides multiple opportunities for students to practice that skill. As students complete these engaging mini-lessons, they will build a repertoire of writing skills they can apply as they write independently during writer's workshop, respond to texts they have read, complete content-area writing assignments, or write to prompts on standardized assessments.

These units are structured around a research-based model-guide-practice-apply approach. You can use these activities in a variety of intervention models, including Response to Intervention (RTI).

Getting Started

In just five simple steps, Everyday Writing Intervention Activities provides everything you need to identify students' needs and to provide targeted intervention.

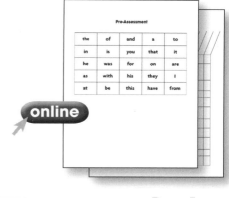

online

1. PRE-ASSESS to identify students'
writing needs. Use the pre-assessment to identify the skills your students need to master.

Day 1

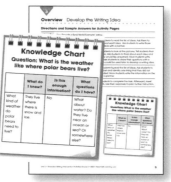

2. MODEL the skill.
Every five-day unit targets a specific writing study area. On Day 1, use the teacher prompts and reproducible activity page to introduce and model the skill.

Day 2

Day 3

Day 4

3. GUIDE, PRACTICE, and APPLY.
Use the reproducible practice activities for Days 2, 3, and 4 to build students' understanding and skill proficiency.

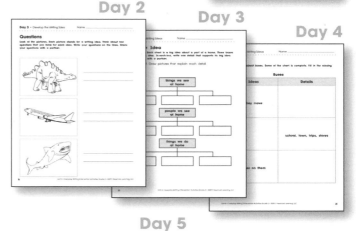

Day 5

4. MONITOR progress.
Administer the Day 5 reproducible assessment to monitor each student's progress and to make instructional decisions.

5. POST-ASSESS to document student progress.
Use the post-assessment to measure students' progress as a result of your interventions.

online

Standards-Based Writing Awareness & Writing Skills in Everyday Intervention Activities

The writing strategies found in the Everyday Intervention Activities series are introduced developmentally and spiral from one grade to the next. The chart below shows the types of words and skill areas addressed at each grade level in this series.

Everyday Writing Intervention Activities Series Skills	K	1	2	3	4	5
Choosing a topic	✔	✔	✔	✔	✔	✔
Narrow the focus	✔	✔	✔	✔	✔	✔
Develop the idea (list what I know, research, complete list)	✔	✔	✔	✔	✔	✔
Organizing ideas/Writing an outline	✔	✔	✔	✔	✔	✔
Strong leads (fiction)	✔	✔	✔	✔	✔	✔
Strong leads (nonfiction)	✔	✔	✔	✔	✔	✔
Developing a character	✔	✔	✔	✔	✔	✔
Developing a plot	✔	✔	✔	✔	✔	✔
Strong endings (fiction)	✔	✔	✔	✔	✔	✔
Strong endings (nonfiction)	✔	✔	✔	✔	✔	✔
What is voice?	✔	✔	✔	✔	✔	✔
How do I write in my voice?	✔	✔	✔	✔	✔	✔
Different voices	✔	✔	✔	✔	✔	✔
Adjectives	✔	✔	✔	✔	✔	✔
Adverbs	✔	✔	✔	✔	✔	✔
Verbs	✔	✔	✔	✔	✔	✔
Nouns	✔	✔	✔	✔		
Advanced nouns					✔	✔
Idioms			✔	✔	✔	✔
Similes			✔	✔	✔	✔
Metaphors					✔	✔
Personification						✔

Everyday Writing Intervention Activities Grade 2 • ©2011 Newmark Learning, LLC

Using Everyday Intervention for RTI

According to the National Center on Response to Intervention, RTI "integrates assessment and intervention within a multi-level prevention system to maximize student achievement and to reduce behavior problems." This model of instruction and assessment allows schools to identify at-risk students, monitor their progress, provide research-proven interventions, and "adjust the intensity and nature of those interventions depending on a student's responsiveness."

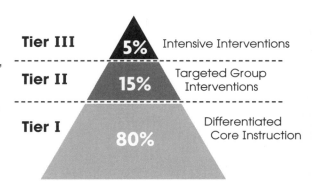

RTI models vary from district to district, but the most prevalent model is a three-tiered approach to instruction and assessment.

The Three Tiers of RTI	Using Everyday Intervention Activities
Tier I: Differentiated Core Instruction • Designed for all students • Preventive, proactive, standards-aligned instruction • Whole- and small-group differentiated instruction • Daily literacy instruction	• Use whole-group writing mini-lessons to introduce and guide practice with vocabulary strategies that all students need to learn. • Use any or all of the units in the order that supports your core instructional program.
Tier II: Targeted Group Interventions • For struggling readers and writers • Provide thirty minutes of daily instruction beyond the Tier I core literacy instruction • Instruction is conducted in small groups of three to five students with similar needs	• Select units based on your students' areas of need (the pre-assessment can help you identify these). • Use the units as week-long, small-group mini-lessons.
Tier III: Intensive Interventions • For high-risk students experiencing considerable difficulty in reading and writing • Provide up to sixty minutes of additional intensive intervention each day in addition to the ninety-minute Tier I core reading instruction • More intense and explicit instruction • Instruction conducted individually or with smaller groups of one to three students with similar needs	• Select units based on your students' areas of need. • Use the units as one component of an intensive reading and writing intervention program.

Overview Choose a Writing Idea

Directions and Sample Answers for Activity Pages

Day 1	See "Provide a Real-World Example" below.
Day 2	Read the title and directions aloud. Give each student a paper bag. Ask students to think about their ideas. Have them answer the questions and share their responses with a partner. Then ask students to decorate their idea bag with pictures that tell about their ideas. Ask students to keep their bags in their desks.
Day 3	Read the title and directions aloud. Place students in pairs and give each student two note cards. Ask students to look at the picture and identify everything about the scene, including people, animals, location, and objects. Suggest that students circle or mark the things they see in the picture. Have students share their thoughts about the picture. Finally, have students choose two ideas about the picture that interest them most, write or draw them on note cards (one idea per card), and place the cards in their idea bags. Remind students that they can use these ideas any time they need a writing topic.
Day 4	Read the title and directions aloud. Give each student two note cards. Have students think about and write or draw two ideas that interest them. Then have pairs share what interests them about each idea. Finally, have students write or draw their ideas on note cards (one idea per note card) and place them in their idea bags.
Day 5	Read the directions aloud. Invite students to choose three ideas that interest them. (If students struggle with adding ideas, provide a few examples for them.) Then ask students to write in the boxes and answer the questions. Discuss their results. Use their responses to plan further instruction and review.

Provide a Real-World Example

◆ Hand out the Day 1 activity page. **Say:** *One of the hardest things a writer has to do is find an idea to write about. How can you tell a good writing idea? Sometimes the things you think about make good ideas for writing. The three important things to remember are to choose an idea that interests you. Choose an idea that you know something about. Choose an idea that you might want to learn more about. These things will help you make a good choice for fiction and nonfiction writing.*

◆ **Say:** *Look at the chart. I wrote three things that interest me. I can't write about all of them. So I will choose one idea that works best for me. I am interested in astronauts but I don't know much about them. I am not interested in learning about them right now.* (Place a Yes and No on the appropriate line.) *My favorite animal is a polar bear. I know something about polar bears and I would like to know more. My garden is another good idea and I do know quite a lot about it. Now I have to choose one! My garden is a great place and I know about it. And being an astronaut is a great idea, but I don't know much about it. I would have to do research to learn all about it. I love polar bears so much and I would like to learn more about them. So I think that I will choose my favorite animal, polar bears, to write about. This took some thinking! Now you think about what you like and what you don't like and what you will enjoy writing about.*

Ideas Chart

Idea	I like this idea.	I know about this idea.	I want to learn more.
astronaut	yes	no	no
polar bears	yes	yes	yes
garden	yes	yes	no

Name _____

Choose an Idea

Complete the chart.

Ideas Chart

Idea	I like this idea.	I know about this idea.	I want to learn more.
astronaut			
polar bears			
garden			

Unit 1 • Everyday Writing Intervention Activities Grade 2 • ©2011 Newmark Learning, LLC

Idea Bag

Complete the activity.

What do you think about?

_____

What are your ideas?

_____

Draw or tell your ideas.

Write "Idea Bag" on the paper bag.
Decorate your bag with pictures to tell about your idea.

Picture of Ideas

Look at the picture. Work with a partner.
Tell about everything you see in the picture.

Choose two ideas from the picture. Write or draw each idea on a card.
Put the card in your Idea Bag.

      Unit 1 • Everyday Writing Intervention Activities Grade 2 • ©2011 Newmark Learning, LLC

Write Your Idea

Think about what interests you. Choose two things.
Write them or draw pictures.

_____

_____

What interests you about each idea?

_____

_____

Write each idea on a note card. Place the note cards in your Idea Bag.

Assessment

Look at the chart. Write three ideas that interest you.
Then answer the questions.

Ideas Chart

Idea	I like this idea.	I know about this idea.	I want to learn more.

Use the chart to answer the questions.

1. Which ideas are good to write about?

2. Which ideas are not good to write about?

3. Which ideas do you need to learn more about? Do you want to learn more about them?

4. Which writing idea do you choose?

Overview   Narrow the Writing Idea

Directions and Sample Answers for Activity Pages

Day 1	See "Provide a Real-World Example" below.
Day 2	Read the title and directions aloud. Invite students to read the list of things to do. Then ask them to organize the list into meaningful groups (such as things to do indoors, things to do outdoors, things to do alone, things to do with friends, things to do with family) and give each group a title. Finally, ask students to think about which group they would like to write about. Ask them to share their thinking with a partner. Remind students that there are many ways to organize the list.
Day 3	Read the title and directions aloud. Ask students to list four things they think of when they see each picture. Remind students that there are no wrong answers. Students will use their ideas in the next lessons.
Day 4	Read the title and directions aloud. Invite students to review their lists from the previous lesson. Ask students to choose one list and organize the list into groups. Give each group a title. Finally, ask students to think about which group they would like to write about, and to share their thinking with a partner.
Day 5	Read the directions aloud. Allow time for students to complete each task. Afterward, meet individually with students to discuss their results. Use their responses to plan further instruction.

Provide a Real-World Example

◆ Hand out the Day 1 activity page. Write "Polar Bears" on the board. **Say:** *I've decided to write about my favorite animal, polar bears. There are so many things about polar bears that I like. How am I going to decide what idea to write about? First, I'll make a list of things that have to do with polar bears.*

◆ Post the list shown here. **Say:** *Wow. That's a long list. And it's not organized. For me to make up my mind, I need to understand what I just wrote. I'm going to put these ideas into groups. I notice that I've listed facts that describe where polar bears live.*

◆ Write words that describe where polar bears live. **Say:** *I've also listed what polar bears look like. I'll write those in another list.* Write words that tell what polar bears look like in another list. **Say:** *I've listed what polar bears eat, too. I'll write those in third list.* Write what polar bears eat in a third list.

◆ **Say:** *Now I need to review each group and label them so I know what the groups are about.* Review and label each group. **Say:** *Now the ideas are organized into categories. Now I need to decide what I'm going to write about. I don't want to write about what polar bears eat or what they look like. I think I really want to write about where they live. Organizing my ideas really helped me make a good decision.*

Polar Bears	Where Polar Bears Live	What Polar Bears Eat	What Polar Bears Look Like
snow	snow	fish	fur looks white
fur	cold	seals	big
white	ice	animals	
cold	ocean		
big			
fish			
ice			
ocean			
animals			
seals			

Narrow the Writing Idea

Write a list of ideas that have to do with polar bears.

Polar Bears

1. _____

2. _____

3. _____

4. _____

5. _____

6. _____

7. _____

8. _____

9. _____

10. _____

Put the ideas into groups. Then give each group a title.

Title: _____   **Title:** _____   **Title:** _____

1. _____   **1.** _____   **1.** _____

2. _____   **2.** _____   **2.** _____

3. _____   **3.** _____   **3.** _____

Let's Organize

Read the list of things to do.

Play a board game

Read a book

Watch television

Skateboard

Make cookies

Swim

Play with my dog

Take a trip

Play soccer

Organize the list into groups. Then give each group a title.

Title: _____ **Title:** _____ **Title:** _____

1. _____ 1. _____ 1. _____

2. _____ 2. _____ 2. _____

3. _____ 3. _____ 3. _____

**Which group would you like to write about most?
Share your thinking with a partner.**

Write Ideas

Look at the pictures. For each picture, write four things that you think about when you look at the picture.

1. _____

2. _____

3. _____

4. _____

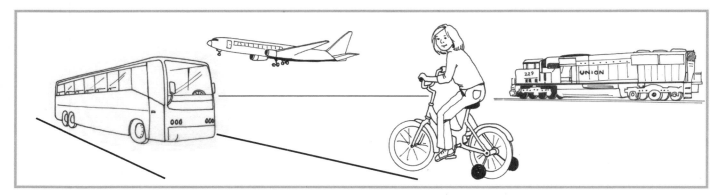

1. _____

2. _____

3. _____

4. _____

Narrow Ideas

Complete the following activity with a partner. Look at your lists from Day 3. Choose one list and put the ideas into two groups. Think about each group. Then give each group a title.

Title: _____

1. _____

2. _____

Title: _____

1. _____

2. _____

Which group would you like to write about?

_____

_____

Assessment

Look at the picture. Write four things that you think about when you see the picture.

1. _____

2. _____

3. _____

4. _____

Put your ideas into groups. Then give each group a title.

Title: _____   **Title:** _____

1. _____   1. _____

2. _____   2. _____

Think about each group. Which group would you like to write about?

_____

Overview Develop the Writing Idea

Directions and Sample Answers for Activity Pages

Day 1	See "Provide a Real-World Example" below.
Day 2	Read the title and directions aloud. Invite students to read the list of ideas. Ask them to identify two things that they already know about each idea. Ask students to write those ideas on the lines provided and to share their ideas with a partner.
Day 3	Read the title and directions aloud. Invite students to look at the pictures. Tell students that each picture stands for a possible writing idea. Ask students to think about each idea and to identify two questions for each idea that they would like answered. Have students write their questions on the lines provided. Finally, ask students to share their questions with a partner. Remind students that each question could be used later to develop a writing idea.
Day 4	Read the title and directions aloud. Invite students to read the list of ideas. Ask students to research each idea using books or the Internet and to identify one thing that they did not know about each idea. Provide help as needed. Have students write the information on the lines provided and share their thoughts with a partner.
Day 5	Read the directions aloud. Allow time for students to complete the task. Afterward, meet individually with students. Discuss their results. Use their responses to plan further instruction.

Provide a Real-World Example

◆ Hand out the Day 1 activity page. **Say:** *I'll use a knowledge chart to help me plan my idea.*

◆ **Say:** *I know from pictures that polar bears live where there is snow. The pictures show them walking on snow. There is usually ice in the pictures, too. These ideas help me know more about the weather where polar bears live. I'll write those things into the chart. Is that all I want to include in my paper? No. That doesn't seem to be enough. So what other questions do I have about polar bears? Well, I think that polar bears eat fish and seals. Does that help me know more about the place where they live? I wonder if that means that they must live near an ocean or sea? I'll write those questions on the chart.*

◆ Circle the last column containing the questions.

◆ **Say:** *I don't have answers to all my questions. I'll need to do a little research on the Internet before I can write my paper. I can probably find information in books also. I will try to find a book on polar bears in the library.*

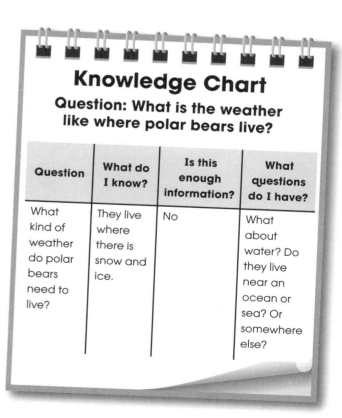

Knowledge Chart

Question: What is the weather like where polar bears live?

Question	What do I know?	Is this enough information?	What questions do I have?
What kind of weather do polar bears need to live?	They live where there is snow and ice.	No	What about water? Do they live near an ocean or sea? Or somewhere else?

Develop the Writing Idea

Listen to your teacher. Then complete the chart below.

Knowledge Chart

Question: What is the weather like where polar bears live?

Question	What do I know?	Is this enough information?	What questions do I have?
What kind of weather do polar bears need to live?			

Name _____

What Do You Know?

Read the list of writing ideas. For each idea, identify two things that you already know. Write your ideas on the lines. Share your information with a partner.

beach

_____

_____

goldfish

_____

_____

farms

_____

_____

Questions

Look at the pictures. Each picture stands for a writing idea.
Think about two questions that you have for each idea.
Write your questions on the lines. Share your questions with a partner.

_____

_____

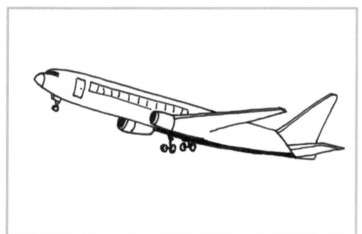

_____

_____

_____

_____

Look It Up

Read the list of ideas from Day 3. Work with a partner to find out one thing that you did not know about each idea. Write the information on the lines.

dinosaur

_____

_____

airplane

_____

_____

shark

_____

_____

Name _____

Assessment

Read the question. Then complete the chart.

Knowledge Chart

Question	What do I know?	Is this enough information?	What questions do I have?
What is fishing?			

Overview Organize Writing Ideas

Directions and Sample Answers for Activity Pages

Day 1	See "Provide a Real-World Example" below.
Day 2	Read the title and directions aloud. Invite students to read each group of words. Tell students that each group tells about, or supports, a big idea about the forest. Ask students to think about the words, decide what the big idea is, and write the idea on the line. Then have students share their thinking with a partner. (Answers: what grows in the forest; what lives in the forest; what there is to do in the forest) Finally, ask students to choose one group of words and illustrate it. Have students share their drawings with a partner.
Day 3	Read the title and directions aloud. Invite students to look at the charts. Explain that each chart is about a different part of a home. Ask students to complete each chart with three details that support each big idea. Have students share their thinking with a partner. Finally, have students choose one chart and illustrate the information in the chart. (Possible answers: books, furniture, television; parents, friends, brothers and sisters; play, read, sleep)
Day 4	Read the title and directions aloud. Have students choose a partner. Invite students to look at the incomplete chart about buses. Ask students to fill in the missing information. (Possible answers: how they move—wheels, motors; where they go—school, town, trips, stores; who rides on them—children, adults, families)
Day 5	Read the directions aloud. Allow time for students to complete the task. (Possible answers: What are deserts?—hot, dry places; Is there water in the desert?—very little; What grows and lives in the desert?—plants and animals). Afterward, meet individually with students. Discuss their results. Use their responses to plan further instruction.

Provide a Real-World Example

◆ Hand out the Day 1 activity page. Review each step and then focus attention on #4.

◆ **Say:** *We have learned a lot about writing. Now we are going to learn how to organize ideas so that we can write things that make sense. What does the word* **organize** *mean?* (Allow responses.)

◆ **Say: Organize** *means to put things in an order that makes sense. When authors write, they organize information in a way that makes sense. They write down big ideas first. Then they write details that support the big ideas. I want to write about where polar bears live. I will organize my information into a chart.*

◆ **Say:** *The first thing I need to do is write down my big ideas. For polar bears, I'm going to choose what weather polar bears need, what polar bears eat, and where polar bears are found. This information will help me know more about where they live.*

◆ **Say:** *My next step is to write these ideas into complete sentences and work on my hook and ending. Remember to plan before you write. It makes writing a little easier.*

Where Polar Bears Live

Big Idea	Details
what weather polar bears need	cold, snowy, icy
what polar bears eat	fish, other animals
where polar bears are found	Arctic, near oceans, near ice

Organize Ideas

1. Choose an idea—polar bears

2. Narrow an idea—where polar bears live

3. Develop an idea—what I know and don't know about where polar bears live

4. Organize ideas to write

Complete the chart.

Big Idea	Details

Big Ideas

Look at each group of words. Each group supports a big idea about a forest. Decide what the big idea is. Write it in the blank.

trees leaves soil seedlings	Big idea: _____ _____
birds squirrels chipmunks insects	Big idea: _____ _____
hiking camping watching birds having a picnic	Big idea: _____ _____

Choose one group of words. Draw a picture that shows the words in the group. Share your drawing with a partner.

Support the Idea

Look at the charts. Each chart is a big idea about a part of a home.
Three boxes are under each big idea. In each box, write one detail
that supports its big idea. Share your thinking with a partner.

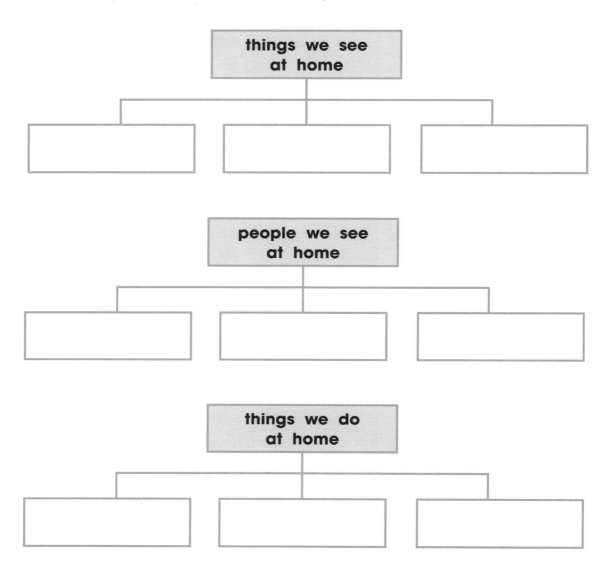

Choose one chart. Draw pictures that explain each detail.

Fill It In

Look at the chart about buses. Some of the chart is complete.
Fill in the missing information.

Buses

Big Idea	Details
how they move	
	school, town, trips, stores
who rides on them	

Assessment

Look at the chart about deserts. Some of the chart is complete.
Fill in the missing information.

Deserts

Big Idea	Details
	hot, dry places
Is there water in the desert?	
	plants, animals

Overview   Strong Fiction Leads

Directions and Sample Answers for Activity Pages

Day 1	See "Provide a Real-World Example" below.
Day 2	Read the title and directions aloud. Invite students to read the leads. Then ask students to analyze the leads and identify which lead they prefer. Finally, have students share their thinking with a partner.
Day 3	Read the title and directions aloud. Invite students to look at the pictures on the left side of the page. Then ask students to match each picture with its correct lead. Ask students to share their results with a partner. (Answers: baby—#3; girl and woman holding hands—#4; kids leaving—#1; baseball game—#2.
Day 4	Read the title and directions aloud. Invite students to look at the pictures. Then ask students to write a strong lead for each picture. If students struggle, have them review leads from Day 3, and offer assistance. Ask students to share their results with a partner.
Day 5	Read the directions aloud. Allow time for students to complete each task. Afterward, meet individually with students to discuss their results. Use their responses to plan further instruction.

Provide a Real-World Example

◆ Hand out the Day 1 activity page. Write the following fiction leads on the board:

> This story is about a noise I heard in the dark. The last thing I wanted to hear was a noise in the dark. But I did.

◆ **Say:** *Good writing often begins with a sentence or two that makes readers want to keep reading. We call these sentences strong leads, or hooks.*

◆ **Say:** *Let's say that I'm going to write a story about a noise I heard one night. I've written two leads and I need to decide which one to choose. Look at the leads on the board.*

◆ Have a student read the leads, and help students analyze them by completing the chart. Use the following information.

◆ **Ask:** *Which lead makes you want to read my story? Why?*

◆ **Say:** *The second lead sounds more interesting than the first. I think my readers will want to find out what the noise was. A strong lead hooks readers this way.*

◆ Remind students that leads like "This story is about . . . " are not strong leads.

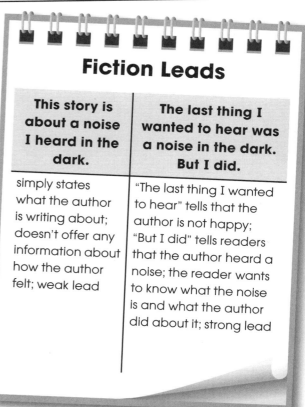

Fiction Leads

This story is about a noise I heard in the dark.	The last thing I wanted to hear was a noise in the dark. But I did.
simply states what the author is writing about; doesn't offer any information about how the author felt; weak lead	"The last thing I wanted to hear" tells that the author is not happy; "But I did" tells readers that the author heard a noise; the reader wants to know what the noise is and what the author did about it; strong lead

Name _____

Strong Fiction Leads

Complete the chart.

Fiction Leads

This story is about a noise I heard in the dark	The last thing I wanted to hear was a noise in the dark. But I did.

Name _____

Strong and Weak Fiction Leads

Read the fiction story leads. Tell which lead is strong and which lead is weak. Use the chart to tell why. Then answer the question.

Dress Up

Leila twirled in front of the mirror. Dressing up was fun!	Leila likes to dress up.

Which lead do you like better? Why?

_____

Last Day of School

"Lots of activities are planned for today," said Rita.	"This is going to be the greatest day ever!" cried Rita.

Which lead do you like better? Why?

_____

Fiction Lead Match-Up

**Look at the pictures. Each picture shows a story idea.
Read the strong fiction leads. Draw a line from the picture
to its matching lead. Share your thinking with a partner.**

<u>**Pictures**</u>

<u>**Strong Fiction Leads**</u>

1. Today I said good-bye
to my two best friends.

2. Some baseball games
are no fun. Today's
game was one of those.

3. "Mom!" Jake shouted.
"He is making a mess
AGAIN!"

4. Days with my Aunt
Marta are the best fun
there is.

Write One

Look at the pictures. Each picture shows a story.
Write a strong story lead for each picture.
Share your leads with a partner.

_____

_____

_____

_____

_____

_____

_____

_____

Assessment

Read the two story leads. Tell which lead is strong and which lead is weak.
Explain what makes each lead strong or weak. Use the chart.

High in the Sky

I live in an apartment.	I live high in the sky. My home is on the 17th floor.

Look at the picture from a story. Write a strong lead for the story.

_____

_____

_____

_____

Overview Strong Nonfiction Leads

Directions and Sample Answers for Activity Pages

Day 1	See "Provide a Real-World Example" below.
Day 2	Read the title and directions aloud. Invite students to look at the chart and read the leads. Then ask students to analyze the leads and identify which lead they prefer. Finally, have students share their thinking with a partner.
Day 3	Read the title and directions aloud. Invite students to look at the pictures on the left side of the page. Then ask students to match each picture with its correct lead. Ask students to share their results with a partner. (Answers: cat carrier—#2; raking leaves—#4; caterpillar—#1; planets—#3)
Day 4	Read the title and directions aloud. Invite students to look at the pictures. Then ask students to write a strong lead for each picture. If students struggle, have them review leads from Day 3, and offer assistance. Ask students to share their results with a partner.
Day 5	Read the directions aloud. Allow time for students to complete each task. Afterward, meet individually with students to discuss their results. Use their responses to plan further instruction.

Provide a Real-World Example

◆ Hand out the Day 1 activity page. **Say:** *When authors write nonfiction, they begin with a sentence or two that makes readers want to keep reading. We call these sentences strong leads, or hooks.*

◆ **Say:** *Let's say that I'm going to write about roller coasters. I've written two leads and can't decide which one to choose. Look at the leads on the board.*

◆ Have a student read the leads and help students analyze them and complete the chart using the following information.

◆ **Ask:** *Which lead makes you want to read my paper? Why?* (Allow responses.)

◆ **Say:** *The second lead sounds more interesting than the first. With the second lead I think my readers will want to read more about roller coasters. Remember to use strong leads to hook your reader.*

◆ Remind students that leads like "This paper is about …" or "I'm going to tell you about a …" are not strong leads.

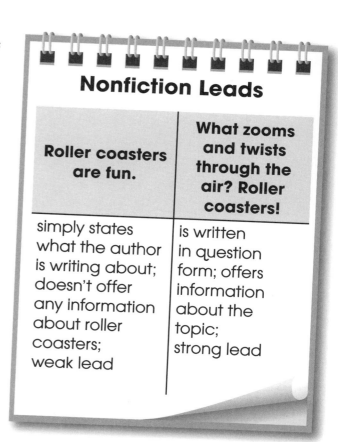

Nonfiction Leads

Roller coasters are fun.	What zooms and twists through the air? Roller coasters!
simply states what the author is writing about; doesn't offer any information about roller coasters; weak lead	is written in question form; offers information about the topic; strong lead

Strong Nonfiction Leads

Complete the chart.

Nonfiction Leads

Roller coasters are fun.	What zooms and twists through the air? Roller coasters!

Strong or Weak?

Read the nonfiction leads. Tell which lead is strong and which lead is weak.
Use the charts to explain why. Then answer the questions.

Earthquake Leads

I'm going to write about earthquakes.	The ground shakes. Rocks break apart. Earthquake!

Which lead do you like better? Why?

_____

Astronaut Leads

Astronauts do many things in space.	What are astronauts doing way up there?

Which lead do you like better? Why?

_____

Name _____

Match-Up

Look at the pictures. Each picture shows a nonfiction writing idea.
Read the nonfiction leads. Draw a line from the picture to its
matching lead. Share your thinking with a partner.

<u>**Pictures**</u>	<u>**Strong Nonfiction Leads**</u>

1. How does a caterpillar become a butterfly?

2. Moving day can be a hard day for pets.

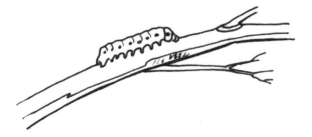

3. Around and around the sun they travel.

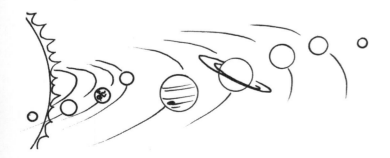

4. There is so much work to be done in the fall.

Write It!

Look at the pictures. Each picture tells a nonfiction writing idea. Write a strong nonfiction lead for each picture. Share your leads with a partner.

_____

_____

_____

_____

_____

_____

_____

_____

Assessment

Read the nonfiction leads. Tell which lead is strong and which lead is weak.
Explain what makes each lead strong or weak.

Fish

Fish swim all day.	Swimming all the day. Always on the go. Fish.

Look at the picture. Write a strong nonfiction lead.

_____

_____

_____

_____

Overview   Develop a Character

Directions and Sample Answers for Activity Pages

Day 1	See "Provide a Real-World Example" below.
Day 2	Read the title and directions aloud. Invite students to look at the pictures and read the sentences. Then ask them to draw how the character changes after the problem occurs. Finally, have students share their drawings with a partner.
Day 3	Read the title and directions aloud. Invite students to look at the two sets of character pictures. Ask students what they think might have happened to change the character. Then ask them to write their ideas on the lines between the two pictures. Finally, have students share their thinking with a partner.
Day 4	Read the title and directions aloud. Invite students to look at the character webs. Ask students to draw pictures of how Henry changes. Remind students to think about how Henry changes over time. Have students share their drawings with a partner.
Day 5	Read the directions aloud. Allow time for students to complete each task. Afterward, meet individually with students to discuss their results. Use their responses to plan further instruction.

Provide a Real-World Example

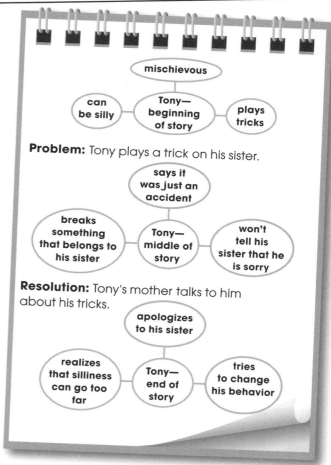

◆ Hand out the Day 1 activity page. **Say:** *Characters are an important part of a story. Good writers think about their characters before they start writing. They decide what their characters will look like and how they will act. These are called character traits. As the story develops, the characters often change traits because of story events.*

◆ **Say**: *This is a character chart on Tony. He's in a story I want to write. I want Tony to be the funny person in the story. He is mischievous, he loves to be silly, and sometimes he plays tricks. When I write my story, I'll be sure to include all of these things and include details that support them.*

◆ Complete the first "Tony" character web. **Say:** *I want my story to be interesting, so I need something to happen. I need a problem. Maybe my problem is that Tony goes too far one day. He plays a trick on his sister and breaks something of hers. This event causes him to change. Help me change Tony in the second character web.*

◆ Help students revise Tony to match the problem. Use information in the second web to develop Tony's character and the information in the third web to redefine Tony's character. **Say:** *Developing a character took some work! When we write we should match a character's actions to what is happening in the story. For a character to develop, the author keeps both character and story events in mind.*

Develop a Character

Complete the character webs.

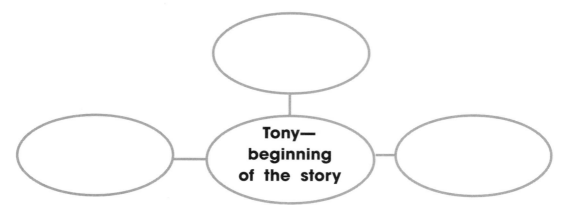

Problem: Tony plays a trick on his sister.

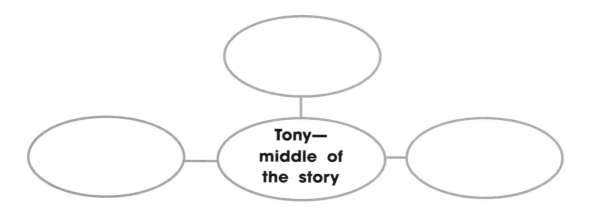

Resolution: Tony's mother talks to him about his tricks.

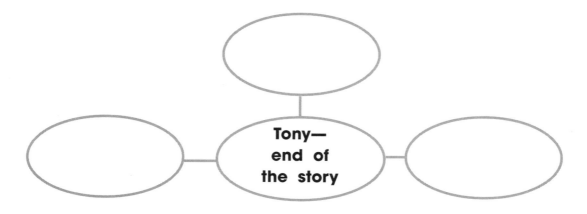

Characters Can Change

Look at the pictures. Read the sentences.
Draw how you think the characters might change.

Problem: Rick runs by. He knocks down the blocks.

Problem: It is Janelle's first day at a new school.
She does not have any friends.

What Happens?

**Look at the pictures. What happens to change the character?
Write your ideas between the pictures.**

_____
_____

_____
_____

More About a Character

**Look at the character webs. They tell how a character named
Henry changes in a story. Think about how each web describes Henry.
Draw pictures that show what you think Henry looks like.**

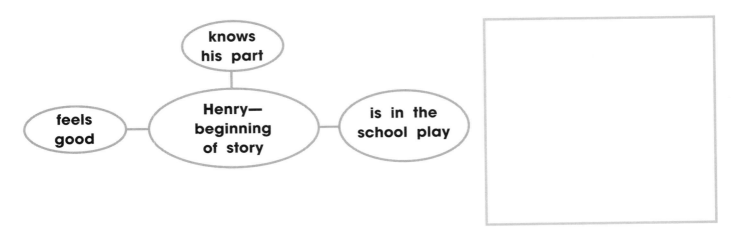

Problem: Henry is standing on stage. He cannot remember his lines.

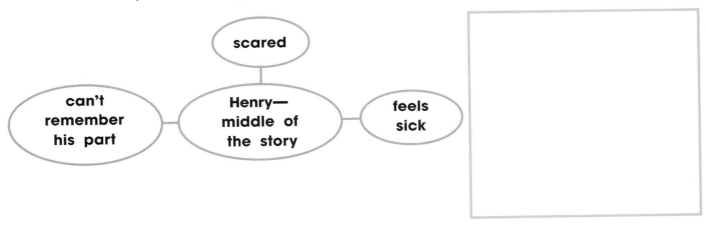

Resolution: Henry remembers his lines. The play ends. People are clapping.

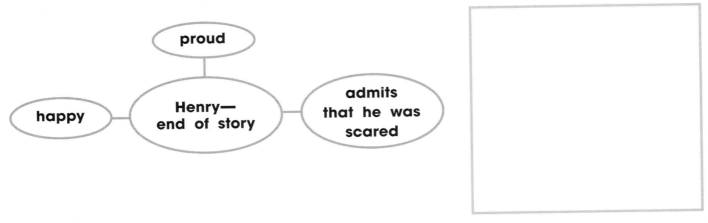

Assessment

Read the first character web. Then fill in the other character webs.

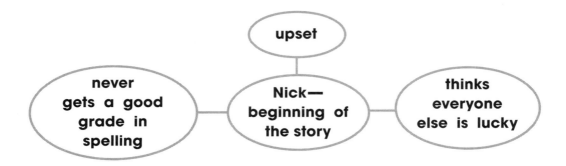

Problem: Nick's friend Nadia gets a good grade in spelling.

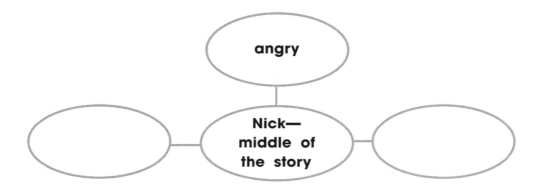

Resolution: Nadia says she studies her spelling words every night.

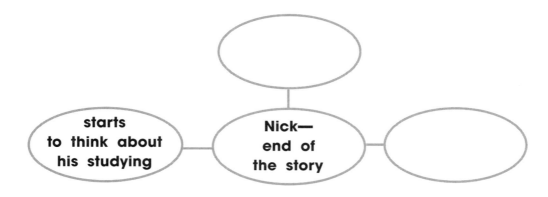

Overview   Develop a Plot

Directions and Sample Answers for Activity Pages

Day 1	See "Provide a Real-World Example" below.
Day 2	Read the title and directions aloud. Invite students to think about a story idea that they might like to write about. Remind students to ask themselves questions like where the story takes place and what the setting looks like. Then ask students to draw the setting. Finally, have students share their drawings with a partner.
Day 3	Read the title and directions aloud. Invite students to read the short stories. Then ask students to complete the stories by drawing the missing event. Finally, have students share their drawings with a partner.
Day 4	Read the title and directions aloud. Invite students to read the story events for the plot. Have students order the events from 1 to 5. Have students share their thinking with a partner. Then have students choose one story event to illustrate. Have students ask a partner to identify which event was illustrated. (Answers: 5, 3, 2, 4, 1)
Day 5	Read the directions aloud. Allow time for students to complete each task. Then meet individually with students to discuss results. Use their responses to plan further instruction.

Provide a Real-World Example

◆   Hand out the Day 1 activity page. **Say:** *The things that happen in a story are called the plot. Good authors spend time thinking about or planning a plot before they start writing. Watch as I develop the plot for the beginning of a story.*

◆   Use the information in the chart to show students how to develop the time, place, and introduction to a short story. **Say:** *The first thing I need to do is decide on my setting, the time and place. I think the time can be the present time. The story will take place in a little girl's room. I will tell something about how the girl's room looks. It will be messy with clothes and books and toys. I think the beginning of my story will be about the young girl getting ready for a birthday party. Now I'll develop the plot for the rest of the story.*

◆   Use the chart to explain that each event connects to the next event and the problem pushes the story. What will the young girl decide about her clothes for the party? The remaining events answer the question.

◆   **Say:** *The last thing I need to do is decide how my story will end. This is called the conclusion. I think the younger sister will do what she wants. Let me write in my conclusion.* Help students analyze the story's conclusion. Point out the ellipses and the word "maybe" indicating that the girl might change her mind. This writing technique leaves a lot to the reader's imagination. **Say:** *Remember that this chart just shows my big events and ideas. To write a really good short story, I need to include details about the setting, the little girl, her sister, and the party. All of these things will keep my readers interested and maybe a little amused.*

Plot Chart

Time	present time right before a birthday party
Place	a little girl's room
Introduction	she is getting ready by herself for a birthday party; she is trying to figure out what to wear; her older sister is going to take her to the party
Story Events (Plot)	1. She dresses in a frilly skirt, a big bow in her hair, sparkly shoes. She is all excited. 2. Her sister tells her that she isn't dressed right; the birthday party is going to be at a playground! She will look silly. 3. She insists that she will wear what she wants. 4. Her excitement fades, but she does not want to change. It is a party and these are party clothes!
Conclusion	She goes back into her room "maybe" to change.

Develop a Plot

Complete the plot chart.

Plot Chart

Time	
Place	
Introduction	
Story Events (Plot)	
Conclusion	

What Is the Setting?

**Think of a story idea to write about. Where and when does
your story take place? What does the place look like? Draw your setting.**

What Is Missing?

Read the stories. One event is missing. Draw the missing event in the box.

Story #1

First event   Jim and Tim race to the playground. They play on the swings and the slide. They have a great time. They do not notice the clouds in the sky.

Second event

Third event   Jim and Tim get home. Their clothes and shoes are wet. Their hair is wet. They drip water on the rug. Mom is not happy.

Story #2

First event   The nest is safe in the tree. There is a lot of noise. "We are hungry," say the baby chicks. They look for Mama Bird.

Second event

Third event   The nest is safe in the tree. There is no noise. The baby chicks are happy.

     Unit 8 • Everyday Writing Intervention Activities Grade 2 • ©2011 Newmark Learning, LLC

What Order?

The story below is about Sam. Read the story events.
They are out of order. Order the events from 1 to 5.

_____ He hears someone call his name. It is his dad.
He is holding Sam's lunch.

_____ He sees that he forgot his lunch!

_____ He goes to his locker. He starts to unpack his backpack.

_____ What should he do? Should he go back home?
Should he call his dad?

_____ Sam arrives at school. He is happy.

Choose one event. Draw a picture of it in the space below. Ask a partner
to choose which event you drew.

Assessment

Read the plot chart. Some information is missing. Complete the chart.

Plot Chart

Time	7:30 a.m. on a school day
Place	Hanna's bedroom
Introduction	The bus is almost here! Hanna cannot find her school project.
Story Events (Plot)	1. She looks on her desk. She looks under the chair. 2. The bus is here. She hears her mother calling. 3. 4.
Conclusion	

Read the story events. An event is missing. Draw the missing event in the box.

First event　Zoe has built the tallest tower! She stops to think. Should she put one more block on the tower?

Second event

Third event　"Well," she says, "I can start all over again."

Overview   Strong Fiction Endings

Directions and Sample Answers for Activity Pages

Day 1	See "Provide a Real-World Example" below.
Day 2	Read the title and directions aloud. Invite students to look at the chart and read the endings. Then ask students to analyze the endings and identify which ending they prefer. Finally, have students share their thinking with a partner.
Day 3	Read the title and directions aloud. Invite students to match each picture with its correct ending. Ask students to share their results with a partner. (Answers: girl dropping biscuits—#3, boy and dad in camp—#1, small girl on stoop—#2)
Day 4	Read the title and directions aloud. Invite students to look at the pictures. Then ask students to write a strong ending for each picture. If students struggle, have them review endings from Day 3, and offer assistance. Ask students to share their results with a partner.
Day 5	Read the directions aloud. Allow time for students to complete the first task. Next, have students complete the second task. Afterward, meet individually with students. Ask them to share responses with you. Discuss their results. Use their responses to plan further instruction.

Provide a Real-World Example

◆ Hand out the Day 1 activity page. **Say:** *Remember that authors often begin their stories with a sentence or two that makes readers want to keep reading. They can do something similar with the endings of their stories. They can end stories with sentences that keep their readers thinking.*

◆ **Say:** *Let's say that I have written a story about a girl named Marley. She's had a difficult day. She had to make an important decision. I've written two endings and can't decide which one to choose. Look at the endings on the board.*

◆ Have one student read the endings. Help students analyze the endings and complete the chart using the following information.

◆ **Ask:** *Which ending makes you think? Why?* (Allow responses.)

◆ **Say:** *The second ending sounds more interesting than the first. The second ending reminds me of what happened to Marley. It also helps me remember that decisions have many results. Just because a decision seems the best on one day does not mean that it is always the best decision.*

◆ Remind students that endings like "My story is done" or "This is the end of my story" are not strong endings.

Fiction Endings

That is the decision Marley made.	That is the decision Marley finally made. But she still has a lot to think about.
simply states how the story ends; doesn't leave the reader thinking; weak ending	summarizes the events; character will think about decision; makes readers think about their own decisions; strong ending

Name _____

Strong Fiction Endings

Listen to your teacher. Then complete the chart.

Fiction Endings

That is the decision Marley made.	That is the decision Marley finally made. But she still has a lot to think about.

Endings—Strong and Weak

These endings complete a story about two boys riding a sled down a small hill. There is a snowman at the bottom of the hill. Read the endings. Tell which ending is strong and which ending is weak. Use the chart.

The Ride

Mel and Jake went around the snowman.	At the last minute Mel and Jake moved to the right. They saved the snowman!

Answer the question. Share your thinking with a partner.

Which ending do you like better? Why?

_____

_____

_____

_____

Matching the Endings

**Look at the pictures. Each picture shows a story.
Read the strong endings. Draw a line from the picture
to its matching ending. Share your results with a partner.**

Pictures   **Strong Fiction Endings**

1. The squirrels plan
to find another home
in the forest.

2. "It's okay, honey,"
said Mom. "Grammy
will be back soon."

3. The puppy grabbed
a biscuit. He hid under
the bed. It was delicious.

End It!

Look at the pictures. Each picture shows a story. Write a strong ending for each picture. Share them with a partner.

_____

_____

_____

_____

_____

_____

_____

_____

Assessment

Read the story endings. Tell which ending is strong and which ending is weak. Explain what makes each ending strong or weak. Use the chart.

The Party

The party was over. It had been fun.	Brenna walked up to her room. She would never forget the party!

Look at the picture from a story. Write a strong ending for the story.

_____

_____

_____

_____

Overview   Strong Nonfiction Endings

Directions and Sample Answers for Activity Pages

Day 1	See "Provide a Real-World Example" below.
Day 2	Read the title and directions aloud. Ask students to analyze the endings and identify which ending they prefer. Have students share their thinking with a partner.
Day 3	Read the title and directions aloud. Invite students to match each picture with its correct ending. Ask students to share their results with a partner. (Answers: family hiking—#2; city street—#1; sun—#4; farmer's market—#3)
Day 4	Read the title and directions aloud. Invite students to look at the pictures. Then ask students to write a strong ending for each picture. If students struggle, have them review endings from Day 3 and offer assistance. Ask students to share their results with a partner.
Day 5	Read the directions aloud. Allow time for students to complete each task. Afterward, meet individually with students to discuss their results and plan further instruction.

Provide a Real-World Example

◆ Hand out the Day 1 activity page. **Say:** *When authors write nonfiction, they begin with a sentence or two that makes readers want to keep reading. They also end with sentences that keep their readers thinking about what they have read.*

◆ **Say:** *Let's say that I'm going to write about recycling. I've written two endings and can't decide which one to choose. Look at the endings on the board.*

◆ Have one student read the endings and help students analyze them and complete the chart using the information here.

◆ **Ask:** *Which ending makes you think about how important recycling is? Why?* (Allow responses.)

◆ **Say:** *The second ending sounds more interesting than the first. Readers might think about recycling because I added a reminder. Remember to use a strong ending to help your readers think.*

◆ Remind students that endings like "This paper was about ..." or "These _____ are wonderful" are not strong endings.

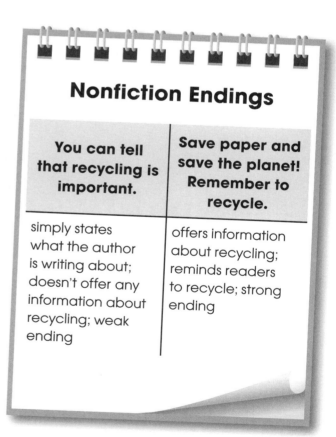

Nonfiction Endings

You can tell that recycling is important.	Save paper and save the planet! Remember to recycle.
simply states what the author is writing about; doesn't offer any information about recycling; weak ending	offers information about recycling; reminds readers to recycle; strong ending

Strong Nonfiction Endings

Complete the chart.

Nonfiction Endings

You can tell that recycling is important.	Save paper and save the planet! Remember to recycle.

Strong or Weak?

Read the nonfiction endings. Tell which ending is strong
and which ending is weak. Explain your thinking. Use the chart.

At the Zoo

The monkeys were the best animals at the zoo.	They played tricks, and made funny faces. No wonder the monkeys were the best animals in the zoo.

Which ending do you like better? Why?

_____

Match It Up

Look at the pictures. Each picture shows a nonfiction writing idea.
Read the nonfiction endings. Draw a line from the picture to its
matching ending. Share your results with a partner.

Pictures   **Strong Nonfiction Endings**

1. Cars and trucks
and buses. The city
is a busy place.

2. That night they were
tired but happy.

3. Support the farmer's
market. Start shopping
there today!

4. The sun is Earth's
special star.

Write One

Look at the pictures. Each picture shows a nonfiction writing idea.
Write a nonfiction ending for each picture. Share your endings with a partner.

_____
_____
_____
_____

_____
_____
_____
_____

Assessment

Read the nonfiction endings. Tell which ending is strong and which ending is weak. Explain your thinking. Use the chart.

On the Ice

The machine cleans the ice. We can skate again.	The skaters return to the ice. And now they can speed along!

Look at the picture and write a strong nonfiction ending.

_____

_____

_____

_____

Overview   What Is Voice?

Directions and Sample Answers for Activity Pages

Day 1	See "Provide a Real-World Example" below.
Day 2	Read the title and directions aloud. Invite students to read the sentences. Ask students to act out how they might really say each sentence. Ask students to choose one sentence and write it as they said it in their own voice.
Day 3	Read the title and directions aloud. Invite students to read the scenes. Ask student pairs to act out what might happen in the scene. If time allows, have student pairs act out one scene for the group.
Day 4	Read the title and directions aloud. Invite students to look at each cartoon and each caption. Ask students to draw lines from each cartoon to its matching caption. (Answer: zoo animals—Big smile; cat and mouse—we just pretend; two frogs—looks GOOD.) Then have students look at each cartoon at the bottom of the page and write a caption for each one.
Day 5	Read the directions aloud. Allow time for students to complete each task. Afterward, meet individually with students to discuss their results. Use their responses to plan further instruction.

Provide a Real-World Example

◆ Hand out the Day 1 activity page. **Say:** *When we write, we want our words to sound like it is us speaking. This is called voice. Think about how you would ask your brother to leave your room. What do you do with the sound of your voice? How do you say the words? Are you going to use a loud voice or a soft voice? How are you going to say something that will make him leave?*

◆ Have students read the first sentence aloud as it is written with no voice. **Say:** *Now say the sentence again, but this time, say it like you are really trying to tell your brother that he has no business in your room. Allow time for students to read the sentence. Talk about the differences.*

What Is Voice?

"Jack! Please! Leave my room! It is my private place."

I can't believe you are late *again*.

Thanks *so much* for the invitation! I can't wait for the party.

You should *really* slow down.

◆ **Say:** *When you read the sentence the second time, I knew you were not simply reading it. I knew you were saying the sentence a certain way. I heard your voices. The way we speak is most often the best way to write. But how would I write that sentence to show my voice coming through? Watch as I rewrite the sentence. (Rewrite as* "Jack! *Please!* Leave my room! It is my private place.")

◆ **Ask:** *Now look at the sentences. I used the word* **please**, *but in a different way. I also added an extra sentence that tells Jack why he has to go. This sounds more like what many of you sounded like. I wrote the sentences in your voice.* Repeat the process with the remaining sentences. Point out the italic words as a useful technique for showing voice.

Voice

Rewrite the sentences using voice.

Jack, please leave my room.

_____

_____

You are late again.

_____

_____

Thank you for the party invitation.

_____

_____

You should slow down.

_____

_____

Act It Out

Read the sentences. Act out how you might say them in real life. Work with a partner.

Shadow is a sweet, gentle dog.

It took me so long to finish this project.

I need a break.

I made a new friend today!

**Choose one sentence. Say it again using voice.
Write the sentence as you said it. Remember that you can
change the way words are spelled and how they look.**

_____

_____

_____

_____

More Voices

Complete the activity with a partner.

Look at the scenes. Act out a short conversation that might happen between the two objects. Work with a partner.

a tall building talking to a short building

_____

_____

a cell phone talking to another cell phone

_____

_____

a computer talking to a printer

_____

_____

a flower talking to a flower pot

_____

_____

Talking

In cartoons, objects can have a voice. Look at the cartoons. Read the captions.
Draw a line from the cartoon to its matching caption.

Cartoons	**Captions**

"I am the one who
looks GOOD."

"Big smile for the
zoo keeper."

"We just pretend not
to like each other."

**Now it's your turn. Look at the cartoons. What might the object
in the cartoon say? Write a caption that shows voice.**

_____

_____

Assessment

Read the sentences. Say them to yourself using your voice. Write the sentence as you said it. Remember that you can change the way words are spelled and the way they look.

I never want to go there again.

_____

_____

May I have another cookie, please?

_____

_____

Look at the scenes. Choose one. Think about what the animal in the cartoon might say. Then write a caption for it.

_____   _____

_____   _____

_____   _____

Overview   Different Voices

Directions and Sample Answers for Activity Pages

Day 1	See "Provide a Real-World Example" below.
Day 2	Read the title and directions aloud. Invite students to read the sentences. Then ask students to think about the audience. Is it the teacher or a sister or brother? Tell students to put T for teacher or S/B for sister or brother. Have students share their answers with a partner. (Answers: 1. T, 2. S/B, 3. S/B, 4. T, 5. S/B, 6. S/B) Then have students write the sentences at the bottom of the page. Remind students to remember their audience.
Day 3	Read the title and directions aloud. Invite students to read the sentences. Then ask students to think about who might say the sentences and write their answers on the lines provided. Finally, have students act out how each person they suggested might say the sentence.
Day 4	Read the title and directions aloud. Invite students to read the sentences in the left-hand column. Then ask students to read the words in the right-hand column. Ask students to think about who the audience for each sentence might be. Have students draw a line matching the sentence on the left with its corresponding audience on the right. Have students share their results with a partner. (Answers: 1. a child, 2. a friend, 3. a teacher, 4. a parent.) Finally, have students choose one sentence and illustrate it.
Day 5	Read the directions aloud. Allow time for students to complete each task. (Answers: 1. a friend, 2. a puppy, 3. children, 4. a parent) Afterward, meet individually with students to discuss their results. Use their responses to plan further instruction.

Provide a Real-World Example

◆ Hand out the Day 1 activity page. Write the postcard notes on the board.

◆ **Ask:** *How do you speak to a friend? How do you speak to an adult? Do you sound the same? Do you use the same words? We often change the way we speak. The way you sound when you talk is called* **voice**. *We use different voices when we write, too. A postcard note to a friend is different than one to an adult relative. Look at the postcard notes on the board.* Have a student read the notes.

◆ **Ask:** *What is different about these two notes? Let's write our thinking on the chart.* (Allow responses.) Use student responses and answers below to complete the chart. *These letters say that the writer is having a good time. But they sound different. They were written to different people so it makes sense that they sound different. They are examples of using different voices for different audiences. What is an audience?* (Allow responses.)

◆ **Say:** *Yes. That's right. An audience is someone who is watching you perform. An audience is also the person who reads what you write. Writing audiences can be a friend, a parent or grandparent, or a teacher. Remember your audience when you write so that you will use the right voice.*

Different Voices

Postcard to a Friend	Postcard to an Adult
says the person's name, uses everyday language, does not describe, signed with the writer's name, sounds friendly	uses Dear, is a little longer, retells events, uses nice language, signed with Love, sounds more like you are talking to an adult relative

Different Voices

Complete the chart.

Different Voices for Different Audiences

Postcard to a Friend	Postcard to an Adult

Carol!

Having a great time.
I have seen some amazing
things. See ya soon!

Kyle

Dear Aunt Lu,

We are all having a good
time. We have been to two
national parks. Some nights
we camp outdoors. It is really
neat. Mom and Dad are
taking a lot of pictures.

Love, Doug

Talking

**Read the sentences. Would you say them to your teacher?
Would you say them to your sister or brother? Write T for teacher
and S/B for sister or brother. Share your answers with a friend.**

_____ 1. I'll be happy to take it to the office.

_____ 2. Sure. Let me have it. I'll give it to him.

_____ 3. I'll be late on Tuesday. And I will miss spelling! Cool.

_____ 4. My mother asked if I could come in late on Tuesday.

_____ 5. Okey-dokey. I'll get it done on time.

_____ 6. They made us finish before we could go out for recess.

   What a pain.

Write a sentence telling your teacher why you are late.

_____

_____

Write a sentence telling your friend that you can go to her party.

_____

_____

Who Is Talking?

Read the sentence.

It is time to come inside.

Who might say this sentence? A sister, a mother, a friend?
Each person would say that sentence using a different voice.

**Read the sentences. Answer the questions. Then act out
the sentences with your partner. Be sure to use voice when
you act out the sentences.**

Please don't make a mess.

Who might say this sentence to you? _____

Who else might say this sentence? _____

Hurry up! I don't want to be late again.

Who might say this sentence to you? _____

Who else might say this sentence? _____

Let's race! First one in the water wins!

Who might say this sentence to you? _____

Who else might say this sentence? _____

Name _____

Who's Listening?

Read the sentences and the audiences. Draw a line from the sentence to its matching audience. Share your answers with a partner.

Sentence	**Audience**
1. I like the way you are behaving.	a friend
2. Can I sit at your table?	a child
3. I am having trouble with my math.	a parent
4. I'm home! Is it time for dinner?	a teacher

Choose one sentence. Draw a picture that includes the audience. Share your picture with a friend.

Assessment

Write a sentence that matches the scene. Remember to use the right voice for the audience.

Tell the teacher that you finished your work.

_____

_____

Tell your puppy that she is a good girl.

_____

_____

Read the audiences in the word bank. Match the audience to the sentence. Write your answer on the line.

Audience Word Bank

a puppy	children	a friend	a parent

I have to go in now and start my homework.

_____

That's a GOOOOOD girl.

_____

It is time for you guys to go to bed.

_____

I am still at practice. So I'll be home a little late.

_____

Overview Adjectives

Directions and Sample Answers for Activity Pages

Day 1	See "Provide a Real-World Example" below.
Day 2	Read the title and directions aloud. Invite students to read the sentences. Then ask them to illustrate what the sentences tell them. Have students share illustrations with a partner.
Day 3	Read the title and directions aloud. Invite students to read the words in the word bank and look at the illustrations. Have students talk about the illustrations with a partner. Then ask students to choose two adjectives from the word bank that describe each illustration and write them on the lines provided. (Answer: #1—worn, torn, #2—cold, snowy, #3 — high, windy) Finally, have students choose one illustration and write a sentence that includes their adjective choices.
Day 4	Read the title and directions aloud. Ask students to revise the sentences by adding an adjective to each sentence. Have students share their revised sentences with a partner.
Day 5	Read the directions aloud. Allow time for students to complete each task. Afterward, meet individually with students to discuss their results. Use their responses to plan further instruction.

Provide a Real-World Example

◆ Hand out the Day 1 Activity page. **Say:** *Writers use special words to tell more about their ideas. They want their readers to really know what they write about. They want readers to see what they see. They use adjectives, or describing words, to tell more about something. Choosing good adjectives can help you do this, too.*

◆ **Say:** *Look at the sentences. Do they tell us anything special about the puppy? Do they help us really see the puppy? No. They just tell us what the puppy did. They don't describe the puppy at all. But by adding some adjectives, I can make the sentences more interesting. I can make them help readers see and hear more about the puppy.*

◆ Write the following revised sentences on the board:

The small puppy ran up to Sis. His wide, round eyes looked up. Then he gave two excited barks and ran off.

◆ **Say:** *Now look at the sentences. I added the adjectives **small**, **wide**, **round**, **two**, and **excited**. How do these adjectives help you know more about the puppy?* (Allow responses.)

◆ Have students copy the revised sentences on the handout. **Say:** *Adjectives describe things. Look at the chart on your handout.* (Review the adjective chart with students.) *Remember, writers want readers to feel something about what they write. Choosing a specific adjective helps them say what they want their readers to see and feel.*

Adjectives

Adjectives describe . . .	Examples
how it looks	small, wide, round, brown
how it sounds	excited, happy, sad
how many	two, many, a few

Adjectives

Rewrite the sentences to include adjectives.

The puppy ran up to Sis. His eyes looked up.
Then he gave a bark and ran off.

_____

_____

Adjectives

Adjectives describe . . .	Examples
how it looks	
how it sounds	
how many	

Pictures Talk

Read the sentences. Draw a picture that shows what the sentence tells you.

He walked into the dark, green forest.

Amy is wearing two pink bows in her curly hair.

The strawberry ice cream cone melted in the yellow sun.

Name _____

Tell About It

Look at the pictures. Choose two adjectives from the word bank that tell about the picture. Write them on the line.

| high | cold | worn | torn | snowy | windy |

_____

_____

_____

_____

_____

_____

Choose one picture. Write a sentence about it.
Use your adjectives. Share your sentence with your partner.

_____

Unit 13 • Everyday Writing Intervention Activities Grade 2 • ©2011 Newmark Learning, LLC

Use the Word

Read the sentences. Revise each sentence by using an adjective.
Share your sentences with a partner.

The bird flew to a nest.

_____

_____

My class visited the zoo.

_____

_____

We love the playground.

_____

_____

Assessment

Read the sentences. Make changes by adding one adjective to each sentence.

The _____ tiger hunted for food.

The little kitten made a _____ mewing sound.

The sailboat flew across the _____ sea.

Look at the picture. Write a descriptive sentence about the picture using adjectives.

_____

_____

Overview   Adverbs

Directions and Sample Answers for Activity Pages

Day 1	See "Provide a Real-World Example" below.
Day 2	Read the title and directions aloud. Invite students to read the sentences. Then ask them to illustrate what the sentences tell them. Have students share their illustrations with a partner.
Day 3	Read the title and directions aloud. Ask students to choose the adverb from the word bank that describes each picture. (Answers: #1—quickly, #2—friendly, #3—gently)
Day 4	Read the title and directions aloud. Ask students to name the adverb in each sentence. Then have them tell whether the adverb tells when, where, or how. (Answers: 1. when, 2. how, 3. where)
Day 5	Read the directions aloud. Allow time for students to complete the first task. (Answers: 1. scary (circled). 2. inside, 3. slowly, 4. then) Next, have students complete the second task. Afterward, meet individually with students. Ask students to share responses with you. Discuss their results. Use their responses to plan further instruction.

Provide a Real-World Example

◆ Hand out the Day 1 activity page. **Say:** *Writers use words to describe the action in their writing. They want readers to see what is happening. Choosing specific adverbs that tell more about the way something happens is one way to do this.*

◆ **Say:** *Look at the sentences on the handout. Do they help us feel anything about the action? Do they help us see what is happening? No, they simply tell what Lisa and her parents are doing and what Lisa knows. These sentences don't describe the action. But by adding a few adverbs, I can make the sentences more interesting and help my readers see the action.*

◆ Write the following revised sentences on the board: Lisa ran quickly toward the finish line. Her parents stood nearby. She knew that the race would be over soon.

◆ **Say:** *Now look at the sentences. I used the adverbs* **quickly**, **nearby**, *and* **soon.** *Each adverb tells more about the action.* **Quickly** *tells how Lisa ran.* **Nearby** *tells where her parents stood and* **soon** *tells when the race would be over.*

◆ Have students copy the revised sentences on the handout.
Say: *Adverbs describe many things. Look at the chart on the handout. Remember, authors want readers to feel something about what they write. Choosing specific adverbs helps them say what they see or feel or what they want their readers to see or feel.*

Adverbs

Adverbs describe . . .	Examples
when	soon, later, yesterday, now
where	nearby, here, there, up, down
how	quickly, harder, carefully, easily, happily

Adverbs

Rewrite the sentences to include adverbs.

Lisa ran toward the finish line. Her parents stood by.
She knew that the race would be over.

_____

_____

Adjectives

Adverbs describe . . .	Examples
when	
where	
how	

Picture It

Read the sentences. Each sentence has an adverb that tells when, where, or how. Under each sentence, draw a picture of what the sentence tells you.

Jay jumped up when he saw the spider.

The ice cream truck stopped in front of the playground.

It would soon be time for school to end.

-ly Adverbs

Look at the pictures. Talk about them with a partner. Then choose the -ly adverb from the word bank that tells about each picture. Write the adverb on the line.

friendly	gently	quickly

_____

_____

_____

_____

_____

_____

Choose one picture. Talk about it with a partner. Write a sentence about it. Be sure to include an adverb.

_____

_____

Tell It

Read the sentences. Tell if the adverb tells where, when, or how.

I will pick up my toys later.

    Later tells _____

I will put some of them neatly on the shelf.

    Neatly tells _____

I will bring the others down to the cellar.

    Down tells _____

Write your own sentence using an adverb.
Then tell if the adverb tells when, where, or how.

_____

_____

Assessment

Complete the activities.

Use the word bank to complete each sentence.
Then circle the answer that is NOT an adverb.

then	scary	slowly	inside

1. She heard a _____ noise.

2. The noise came from _____ the closet.

3. She walked _____ toward the closet.

4. _____ she heard the noise grow louder!

Look at the pictures. Write a sentence using adverbs for each picture.

_____

_____

_____

_____

_____

_____

Overview   Strong Verbs

Directions and Sample Answers for Activity Pages

Day 1	See "Provide a Real-World Example" below.
Day 2	Read the title and directions aloud. Invite students to read the sentence pairs with a partner and decide which sentence contains the strong verb. Have students circle the sentence containing the strong verb. (Answers: 1. crash, 2. inspects, 3. grabs) Then have students choose one sentence and draw a picture to tell about it.
Day 3	Read the title and directions aloud. Invite students to read the words in the word bank and the sentences. Have students choose the strong verb that completes the sentence and write it on the line provided. (Answers: 1. exclaimed, 2. cried, 3. ordered, 4. begged) Finally, have students choose one sentence and illustrate it.
Day 4	Read the title and directions aloud. Invite students to read the verbs in each column. Then ask students to draw a line from the weak verb to its matching stronger verb. Have students choose one strong verb and use it in a sentence. (Answers: walk/hike, make/build, hit/smack, say/shout)
Day 5	Read the directions aloud. Allow time for students to complete each task. (Answers: 1. pleaded, 2. flew, 3. glared) Afterward, meet individually with students to discuss their results. Use their responses to plan further instruction.

Provide a Real-World Example

◆ Hand out the Day 1 activity page. **Say:** *Writers use verbs to tell what is happening in their writing. Choosing strong verbs can make writing come alive.* **Say:** *Look at the sentences. Do they paint a lively picture of the scene? Not really. They just tell us what happened without adding anything exciting. The writing does not come alive. But by changing a few of the verbs, I can make the sentences more interesting and help my readers see the scene.*

◆ Rewrite the sentences on the board using strong verbs, such as: Tasha grabbed the torn slipper from the puppy.; She glared at him.; She shouted at him.; He was sneaking toward the door.; Then he escaped.

◆ **Say:** *Now look at the sentences. Can you picture Tasha grabbing the torn slipper? I changed the verbs* **took**, **looked**, **talked**, *and* **moving**, *and* **went** *with the strong verbs* **grabbed**, **glared**, **shouted**, **sneaking**, *and* **escaped**. *These verbs give a better picture of what is happening. How did the changes affect what you thought was happening in the writing?* (Allow responses.)

◆ Have students copy the revised sentences on the handout. **Say:** *Writers want readers to see what is happening in their writing. Choosing strong verbs helps them show what is happening and makes it come alive to readers.*

Strong Verbs

Verb	Strong Verb
took	grabbed, snatched
looking	glared, stared
talked	shouted, screeched
moving	sneaking, creeping
went	escaped

Strong Verbs

Rewrite the sentences to include strong verbs.

Tasha took the torn slipper from the puppy.

_____

_____

She looked at him.

_____

_____

She talked to him.

_____

_____

He was moving toward the door.

_____

_____

Then he went out!

_____

Act Out a Verb

Read each sentence pair. Act out each sentence.
Circle the sentence with the strong verb.

1. Huge waves move against the sand.

   Huge waves crash against the sand.

2. The man inspects each bag.

   The man looks inside each bag.

3. Susan takes her bag of popcorn.

   Susan grabs her bag of popcorn.

Choose one sentence. Draw a picture of what it tells.
Use the strong verb to help you.

"Said" Verbs

There are many ways to say "said." Read the sentences.
Choose a word from the word bank to complete each sentence.
Share your revised sentences with a partner.

ordered	exclaimed	begged	cried

"Finally! I found some peanut butter and jelly," _____

Manny.

"Oh, no! I can't eat that again!" _____ Sam.

"You have to eat what I eat," _____ Manny.

"Please," _____ Sam.   "No more peanut butter and jelly."

Choose one sentence and draw a picture of it.
Share your picture with your partner.

Choose a Verb

Read each column. Draw a line from the weak verb to its matching strong verb.

Weak Verbs	**Strong Verbs**
walk	hike
make	shout
hit	smack
say	build

Choose one strong verb. Use it in a sentence or draw a picture that tells about it.

_____

_____

Assessment

Read the sentences. Choose a strong verb from the word bank. Use it to complete each sentence.

glared	flew	pleaded

1. "Come right away. We need help," the twins _____.

2. The baseball _____ out over the field.

3. Mr. Baker _____ at the children in the back row.

Read the sentences. Replace the weak verb with a strong verb.

1. The girls <u>call</u> to each other across the playground.

2. Every year Jen <u>gets</u> a first prize at the fair.

_____

_____

Overview   Nouns

Directions and Sample Answers for Activity Pages

Day 1	See "Provide a Real-World Example" below.
Day 2	Read the title and directions aloud. Ask students to draw lines matching the noun on the left side with its synonym on the right side. Have students share responses with a partner. Finally, have students choose one new noun and use it in a sentence. (Answers: fight/battle, place/spot, ocean/sea, group/team, plant/flower)
Day 3	Read the title and directions aloud. Invite students to read the sentences. Ask students to choose nouns from the word bank that mean about the same thing as the boldfaced words. Have students rewrite the sentences using the new nouns. (Answers: 1. home, 2. pond, 3. bear, 4. task) Finally, ask students to choose a sentence and illustrate it.
Day 4	Read the title and directions aloud. Invite students to read the nouns in both columns. Then ask students to draw lines matching food groups on the left side with their food words on the right side. Have students choose one food word and use it in a sentence. (Answers: vegetable/lettuce, fruit/apple, meat/hamburger, dairy/milk, grain/cereal)
Day 5	Read the directions aloud. Allow time for students to complete the first task. (Answers: dish—plate, ground—earth, rain—storm) Next, have students complete the second task. (Answers: 1. desk, 2. path, 3. Ben) Afterward, meet individually with students. Ask students to share responses with you. Discuss their results. Use their responses to plan further instruction.

Provide a Real-World Example

◆ Hand out the Day 1 activity page. **Ask:** *Sister, school, table, happiness: What can you tell about these words?* (Allow responses.)

◆ **Say:** *Yes. They are all nouns. Nouns name a person, place, thing, or idea. What are some person nouns?* (Allow responses.) If students struggle, suggest nouns from the chart here. Repeat with place, thing, and idea nouns.

◆ Complete the sentence: I had to help Lisa get ready. She is just a little <u>girl</u>.

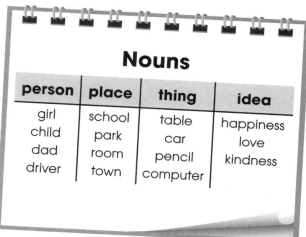

Nouns

person	place	thing	idea
girl	school	table	happiness
child	park	car	love
dad	room	pencil	kindness
driver	town	computer	

◆ **Say:** *Good authors want to use the noun that tells exactly what they are thinking. Let's think about how to use the best noun. Look at the second sentence. The word **girl** is a great noun. Readers know what a girl is, but the sentence is about a very young girl. Right? So I wonder if there is another noun that we could use in place of girl. A noun that means someone very young. Another word for a young girl.*

◆ Write the following revised sentences on the board. Underline **child**. I had to help Lisa get ready. She is just a little <u>child</u>. **Say:** *Now look at the sentence. I changed **girl** to **child**. What do you think of when you hear the word **child**?* (Allow responses.) **Say:** *Girl and child tell the same thing. In this case, child might be the better word to use. Remember, authors choose words that tell exactly what they feel. They think about what they really want to say and use the best words to say it. In this unit, you will learn some of the best words to use in your writing.*

Nouns

Complete the sentences.

I had to help Lisa get ready. She is just a little _____ .

I had to help Lisa get ready. She is just a little _____ .

Think of examples to complete the chart.

Nouns

person	place	thing	idea

Match the Nouns

Read the nouns in both columns. Find nouns with the same meaning. Draw lines matching nouns from the first column to the nouns in the right column. Share your thinking with a partner.

<u>Group 1</u>	<u>Group 2</u>
fight	team
place	spot
ocean	battle
group	flower
plant	sea

Choose a noun from Group 2 and write a sentence using it.

_____

_____

Choose a Noun

**Read the sentences. Choose nouns from the word bank
that mean about the same thing as the boldfaced nouns.
Rewrite the sentences using your new nouns.
Share your sentences with a partner.**

task	home	bear	pond

1. Julie likes to stay in her own **house**.

2. The beaver plays in the **water**.

3. Ken loves his old stuffed **animal**.

4. My first **job** is to teach my students.

Choose a sentence and draw a picture of it.

Food Nouns

Complete the activity with a partner. Vegetable or fruit?
Meat or grain? These are nouns that tell about food groups.
Read the list of food groups in column one. Then read the food words
in column two. Draw lines matching the food group to the food word.

Food Groups	**Food Words**
vegetable	hamburger
fruit	milk
meat	apple
dairy	cereal
grain	lettuce

Choose one food word. Use it in a sentence.

_____

_____

Assessment

Read the nouns in both columns. Draw lines matching nouns from Group 1 to nouns in Group 2.

<u>**Group 1**</u>   <u>**Group 2**</u>

dish   earth

ground   storm

rain   plate

Read the sentences. Look at the boldfaced noun. Choose a noun from the word bank that means about the same thing. Rewrite the sentences using your new noun.

Ben	desk	path

1. Please sit quietly at your **seat**.

_____

2. This is the **way** we need to walk.

_____

3. I know that **he** will arrive any minute.

_____

Overview Idioms

Directions and Sample Answers for Activity Pages

Day 1	See "Provide a Real-World Example" below.
Day 2	Read the title and directions aloud. Ask students to draw a line matching the sentence on the left with its corresponding sentence on the right. Have students share their results with a partner. (Answers: 1. I decided to work very hard. 2. People are sure to buy these toys. 3. We share the same problem today. 4. I forget my troubles when I am away.)
Day 3	Read the title and directions aloud. Invite students to read the sentences. Ask students to tell what each sentence means. Then have students draw a picture illustrating one sentence. Have students share thinking and illustration with a partner. (Answers: 1. It is time to give up. 2. Let's get going. 3. Tell how you feel. 4. That meal tasted terrific.)
Day 4	Read the title and directions aloud. Have students read the sentences. Then have students match the sentences to the idioms in the bank. Have students share their thinking with a partner. (Answer: 1. hold your horses, 2. start the ball rolling, 3. face the music, 4. ball of fire) Finally, have students choose one idiom and use it in a sentence.
Day 5	Read the directions aloud. Allow time for students to complete the first task. (Answers: 1. raining heavily, 2. stopped suddenly and stood motionless.) Then ask students to complete the second task. (Answers: 1. go all out, 2. pulling my leg, 3. put our heads together) Afterward, meet individually with students to discuss their results. Use their responses to plan further instruction.

Provide a Real-World Example

◆ Hand out the Day 1 activity page. **Say:** *Authors often try to create pictures in the minds of their readers. Using idioms is one way to do this. An idiom is a way that people talk and write. What they say isn't really what they mean. You have to know the idiom to know what the author means. Let's learn about idioms. Read the first sentence. I can rewrite that sentence using an idiom. I will try to create a picture in the reader's mind.*

◆ Revise the sentence with the example below. **Say:** *Now read the sentence. There are no cats or dogs outside. The idiom "raining cats and dogs" means that it is raining a lot. It is pouring rain. Let's look at a few other idioms.*

◆ Write the next sentence on the board.

◆ **Ask:** *What does this sentence say?* (Allow responses.) *Yes. That's right. It says that it is time to quit work. Now look at the sentence with an idiom in it.*

◆ Revise the sentence with the examples below.

◆ **Say:** *No one is calling a day anything. That's just a phrase, or idiom, people use to say that it is time to stop.*

◆ Repeat with the remaining examples.

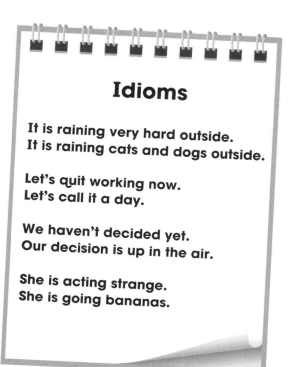

Idioms

It is raining very hard outside.
It is raining cats and dogs outside.

Let's quit working now.
Let's call it a day.

We haven't decided yet.
Our decision is up in the air.

She is acting strange.
She is going bananas.

Idioms

Rewrite the sentences using idioms.

1. It is raining very hard outside.

_____

_____

2. Let's quit working now.

_____

_____

3. We haven't decided yet.

_____

_____

4. She is acting strange.

_____

_____

Name _____

Idiom Match

Read the sentences in both columns. The sentences in column one have idioms. The sentences in column two have the same meaning. Draw a line from the idiom sentence to the meaning sentence.

Idiom Sentences

1. I decided to go all out.

2. These toys should sell like hotcakes.

3. We are in the same boat today.

4. Out of sight, out of mind.

Plain Sentences

People are sure to buy these toys.

We share the same problem today.

I forget my troubles when I am away.

I decided to work very hard.

Choose one of the idiom sentences and draw what it looks like to you. Ask a partner to choose which sentence you drew.

Tell What It Means

Read the sentences. Look at the underlined idiom. Tell what each sentence really means. Then draw a picture describing one sentence. Share your thinking and drawing with a partner.

1. I just can't do it. It's time to <u>throw in the towel</u>.

_____

_____

2. We are late. Let's <u>get this show on the road</u>!

_____

_____

3. You look upset. Maybe you should <u>blow off some steam</u>.

_____

_____

4. Mom! That meal really <u>hit the spot</u>.

_____

_____

Name _____

Write Some Idioms

Read the sentences. What idiom could you use for each sentence?
Choose one from the idiom bank. Write it on the line.
Share your answers with a partner.

| start the ball rolling | face the music | hold your horses | a ball of fire |

1. Wait! You need to stop.

_____

2. I think that Burt should go first.

_____

3. We need to just get it over with.

_____

4. My youngest child is full of energy.

_____

Choose one idiom from the bank and use it in a sentence.

_____

Assessment

Read the sentences. Look at the underlined idiom phrase.
Tell what each sentence really means.

1. It's raining cats and dogs outside.

_____

_____

2. He took one look at the tiger and stopped dead in his tracks.

_____

_____

Read the sentences. What idiom could you use for each sentence?
Choose one from the idiom bank and write it on the line.

pulling my leg	put our heads together	go all out

1. Let's really do our best.

_____

2. You are teasing me.

_____

3. We should work to plan a great party.

_____

Overview   Similes

Directions and Sample Answers for Activity Pages

Day 1	See "Provide a Real-World Example" below.
Day 2	Read the title and directions aloud. Invite students to read the sentences. Ask students to tell what is being compared. Then have them draw a picture illustrating the sentence. Have students share their thinking and illustrations with a partner. (Answers: 1. hat and feather; 2. children and gold; 3. touch and rain)
Day 3	Read the title and directions aloud. Invite students to read the sentences. Ask students to tell what is being compared. Then have them draw a picture illustrating the sentence. Have students share their thinking and illustrations with a partner. (Answers: 1. coat and a glove; 2. Gregg and a horse; 3. Spot and a bump on a log)
Day 4	Read the title and directions aloud. Ask students to draw a line matching each sentence on the left with its corresponding sentence on the right. (Answers: 1. His eyes flash like fire. 2. She is as busy as a bee. 3. He swims like a fish. 4. I am as hungry as a bear.) Then have students choose one sentences from the right side, tell what is being compared, and illustrate it. Have students share their thinking and illustrations with a partner.
Day 5	Read the directions aloud. Allow time for students to complete the task. (Answers: 1. the children and mice. The children are very quiet. 2. The floor and a rock. The floor is hard. 3. Molly and Annie to cats and dogs. Molly and Annie fight a lot.) Afterward, meet individually with students. Ask students to share responses with you. Discuss their results. Use their responses to plan further instruction.

Provide a Real-World Example

◆ Hand out the Day 1 activity page. **Say:** *Authors want to create pictures in the minds of their readers. Using similes is one way to do this. A simile compares two things using the words* **like** *or* **as**. *Read the sentence on the board. I think I can rewrite that sentence using a simile. I think it will create a picture in the reader's mind.*

◆ Revise the sentence with the example shown. **Say:** *Now read the sentence. I compared Jake to a lion using the word* **as**. *I'm still saying that Jake is brave. But now I'm saying it in a more colorful, interesting way. You can draw a picture in your mind of Jake being very brave. Let's look at another simile example.*

◆ Write the next sentence on the board.

◆ **Say:** *This sentence says that Jake runs fast. But what does Jake look like? Watch as I revise this sentence and put a simile in it.*

◆ Then encourage students to write their own similes using **like** or **as**.

Similes

Jake is very brave.

Jake is as brave as a lion.

Jake runs fast.

Jake runs like the wind.

Similes

Rewrite the sentences to include similes. Tell what is being compared. Then draw a picture to show what the sentence is telling you.

Jake is very brave.

_____

_____

What is being compared?

_____

Jake runs fast.

_____

_____

What is being compared?

_____

A Picture

Read the sentences using "as" similes. Tell what is being compared.
Then draw a picture showing what the sentence tells you. Share with a partner.

1. This hat is as soft as a feather.

What is being compared?

_____

_____

2. The children are as good as gold.

What is being compared?

_____

_____

3. Her touch is as gentle as the rain.

What is being compared?

_____

_____

Name _____

More Pictures

**Read the sentences using "like" similes. Tell what is being compared.
Then draw a picture showing what the sentence tells you.
Share with a partner.**

1. Becca has a new coat.
   It fits like a glove.

What is being compared?

_____

_____

2. Gregg was so hungry
   he ate like a horse.

What is being compared?

_____

_____

3 Spot refused to move.
   He sat like a bump on a log.

What is being compared?

_____

_____

Match the Similes

Read the sentences in both columns. The sentences in the first column do not have similes. The sentences on the right do have similes. Draw a line to match the sentences.

1. His eyes are bright.   **He swims like a fish.**

2. Paula works all the time.   **I am as hungry as a bear.**

3. Bob swims fast.   **His eyes flash like fire.**

4. I am really hungry.   **She is as busy as a bee.**

Choose one sentence from the right side. Tell what two things are being compared. Draw a picture showing what the sentence really means.

Assessment

**Read the sentences. Tell what is being compared.
Then tell what the sentences really mean.**

1. The children are as quiet as mice.

What is being compared?

_____

What does the sentence mean?

_____

_____

2. I can't sit on the floor. It is as hard as a rock.

What is being compared?

_____

What does the sentence mean?

_____

_____

3. What can we do? Molly and Annie fight like cats and dogs.

What is being compared?

_____

What does the sentence mean?

_____

_____

Overview   What Is a Sentence?

Directions and Sample Answers for Activity Pages

Day 1	See "Provide a Real-World Example" below.
Day 2	Read the title and directions aloud. Invite students to read each group of words. Ask students to decide if each group is a sentence fragment or a complete sentence. Have students label sentence fragments with an "F" and complete sentences with a "C." Have students share responses. Finally, ask students to rewrite sentence fragments into complete sentences and share their new sentences with a partner. (Answers: 1. C, 2. F, 3. F, 4. C)
Day 3	Read the title and directions aloud. Invite students to read each sentence fragment and rewrite the fragments into complete sentences. Finally, ask students to choose one new sentence and illustrate it.
Day 4	Read the title and directions aloud. Invite students to read the sentence fragments in both columns. Ask students to make complete sentences by drawing lines from fragments in the left column to fragments in the right column. Finally, have students choose two sentences and illustrate them. Have students share their illustrations with a partner. (Answers: My little brother tore my homework. Our neighbor's cat caught a mouse. Do not mess with a bear's den. Can you bring cupcakes to school?)
Day 5	Read the directions aloud. Allow time for students to complete the task. (Answers: 1. F, 2. C, 3. F, 4. C) Next, have students complete the second task. Afterward, meet individually with students. Discuss their results. Use their responses to plan further instruction.

Provide a Real-World Example

◆ Hand out the Day 1 activity page. Show students a large piece of an eggshell. **Ask:** *What am I holding in my hand?* (Allow responses.) **Say:** *Yes. I'm holding a piece of an eggshell. This is an eggshell* **fragment**. *The word* **fragment** *means not complete, or incomplete. A complete eggshell has all the pieces.* Write the word **fragment** under the picture of an eggshell fragment. Write the word **complete** under the picture of a complete eggshell.

◆ **Say:** *I think of an eggshell when I think of sentences. Authors put words together to make a sentence, but how does an author know a sentence is complete? To answer that question, I need to know what a sentence is. A sentence is a group of words that answers two questions: Who or what is the sentence about? and What happened in the sentence? We know that the* who or what *of a sentence is the noun: the person, place, thing, or idea. What happened in a sentence is the verb, or action.*

◆ Write a sentence fragment on the board. Then practice making fragments into sentences. **Say:** *If the words don't answer both questions, then it is a sentence fragment. How can we make this a sentence?* (Allow responses.)

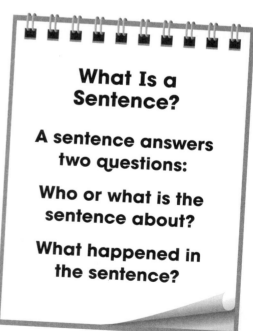

What Is a Sentence?

A sentence answers two questions:

Who or what is the sentence about?

What happened in the sentence?

What Is a Sentence?

Listen to you teacher. Then rewrite the fragments to make sentences.

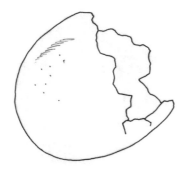   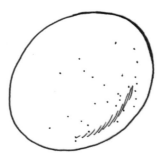

_____   _____

an eggshell

_____

_____

sits on the front porch

_____

_____

my ice cream cone

_____

_____

slipped

_____

_____

Fragment or Not?

Read each group of words. Put an "F" by the words that are sentence fragments. Put a "C" by the words that are complete sentences. (Clue: There are two sentence fragments and two complete sentences.) Share your answers with a partner.

☐ I spilled water on my book.

☐ Hot outside.

☐ Hit ball.

☐ The bird flew from the cage.

Rewrite the sentence fragments into complete sentences. Share your sentences with a partner.

_____

_____

_____

Rewrite Fragments

**Read each sentence fragment. Rewrite the words into sentences.
Remember to add details, capital letters, and periods.**

1. some people

_____

_____

2. runs in the race

_____

_____

3. found a home

_____

_____

4. the spider

_____

_____

Choose one sentence. Draw a picture of the sentence.

Fragment Match-Up

Read the sentence fragments in both columns. Make complete sentences by drawing lines from the fragments in the left column to fragments in the right column. Share your answers with a partner.

Who or What?	**What Happened?**
My little brother	a bear's den.
Our neighbor's cat	tore my homework.
Do not mess with	cupcakes to school?
Can you bring	caught a mouse.

Choose two sentences. Draw a picture for each sentence.
Share your drawings with a partner. Can your partner guess
which sentences you drew?

Assessment

Read each group of words. Put an "F" by the words that are sentence fragments. Put a "C" by the words that are complete sentences.

☐ Made a cake.

☐ John painted birdhouses.

☐ Our football team.

☐ The glass lamp broke.

Read each sentence fragment. Rewrite the words into complete sentences. Remember to add details, capital letters, and periods.

1. the grass

_____

_____

2. jumped out of the box

_____

_____

Overview   Varying Sentence Structure

Directions and Sample Answers for Activity Pages

Day 1	See "Provide a Real-World Example" below.
Day 2	Read the title and directions aloud. Invite students to read each sentence and question. Tell them that the answer to each question adds detail to each sentence. Have students rewrite the sentence and include the answer to the question. Finally, have students choose one sentence and illustrate it.
Day 3	Read the title and directions aloud. Invite students to read the sentences in the sentence bank. Then ask students to read the sentence pairs. Have students match sentence pairs to the correct sentence in the bank and write it on the line. Finally, ask students to illustrate each answer.
Day 4	Read the title and directions aloud. Invite students to read the sentence pairs. Ask students to combine pairs into one sentence. Have students choose one combined sentence and illustrate it. If students struggle, have them review sentences from Day 3. (Possible answers: The boy laughed and fell off the bunk bed. The crooked tree is dead. Dad mowed the grass in the rain. The car was in the garage because it had a flat tire.)
Day 5	Read the directions aloud. Allow time for students to complete the task. (Possible answers: Michael fell in the dirt. The butterfly flew away because of the rain.) Then have students complete the second task. (Possible answers: My aunt loves cookies and hamburgers. The boys found pretty shells on the beach.) Afterward, meet individually with students. Discuss their results. Use their responses to plan further instruction.

Provide a Real-World Example

◆ Hand out the Day 1 activity page. Have a student read the paragraph. **Ask:** *What is this paragraph about?* (Allow responses.) *What does this paragraph tell us about snow?* **Say:** *This paragraph gives good information about snow, but it doesn't sound very interesting. What do you notice about the sentences?* (Allow responses.)

◆ **Say:** *Yes. The sentences look alike, or similar. One way that authors make their writing interesting is to change the way their sentences look. Most of these sentences start with "it is" or "it does." I bet I can make this paragraph more interesting. I can do that three different ways. I can start sentences with different words. I can combine short sentences, and I can add details.* Point out the ways on the chart here to change sentences on the activity page.

◆ **Say:** *Watch as I rewrite this paragraph. I'll keep my first sentence the same.* Combine the next two sentences and add a sentence to the end. **Say:** *Now look at my paragraph. It's definitely longer, but it also says more about snow.*

◆ Have students copy the revised paragraph on their handout and then share other possibilities.

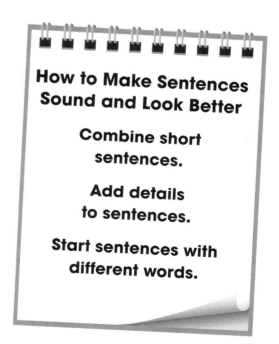

How to Make Sentences Sound and Look Better

Combine short sentences.

Add details to sentences.

Start sentences with different words.

Varying Sentence Structure

Rewrite the following paragraph.

Snow is very interesting. It is cold. It is wet.
It does not snow everywhere. It is fun.

_____

_____

_____

_____

_____

_____

_____

Add Detail

Read each sentence. Read the question after each sentence.
Add details to the sentence to answer the question.
Rewrite the sentence on the lines.

1. My cat slept. (Where did the cat sleep?)

_____

_____

2. John ran. (When did John run?)

_____

_____

3. Amy was mad. (Why was Amy mad?)

_____

_____

4. It was raining outside. (What did you do because it was raining outside?)

_____

_____

Choose one sentence that you have changed.
Draw a picture of the sentence.

Sentence Match-Up

Read the sentence pairs. Read the sentences in the sentence bank.
Match the sentence pairs with the correct combined sentence.
Write the correct combined sentence on the lines. Share your results
with a partner. Finally, draw pictures for your new sentences.

My brother John goes to college.	The cat jumped out of the tree and ran to the backyard.	The tall glass is green.	It was hot when the parade started at ten o'clock.

The cat jumped out of the tree.
The cat ran to the backyard.

_____

_____

John is my brother. He goes to college.

_____

_____

The parade started at ten o'clock.
It was very hot when the parade started.

_____

_____

The glass is tall. The glass is green.

_____

_____

Combining Sentences

Read the sentences. Combine them into one sentence.

1. The boy laughed. The boy fell off the bunk bed.

_____

_____

2. The tree is crooked. The tree is dead.

_____

_____

3. Dad mowed the grass. It was raining.

_____

_____

4. The car was in the garage. The car had a flat tire.

_____

_____

Choose one combined sentence and draw a picture of it.

Assessment

Read each sentence. Read the question after each sentence.
Add details to the sentence that answer the question.
Rewrite the sentence on the lines.

1. Michael fell. (Where did Michael fall?)

   _____

   _____

2. The butterfly flew away. (Why did the butterfly fly away?)

   _____

   _____

Read the sentences. Combine them into one sentence.
Share your sentence with a partner.

1. My aunt loves cookies.

   My aunt loves hamburgers.

   _____

   _____

2. The boys found shells on the beach.

   The shells were pretty.

   _____

   _____

Notes

Notes